Ornate Persona

Jeanine Stevens

Clare Songbirds Publishing House Poetry Series
ISBN 978-1-957221-03-8
Clare Songbirds Publishing House
Ornate Persona © 2022 Jeanine Stevens

Printed in the United States of America
FIRST EDITION

140 Cottage Street
Auburn, New York 13021
www.claresongbirdspub.com

Clare Songbirds
Publishing House

Contents

Acknowledgements

Arabesque: "Why Dancers Wear White," "The Blueberry Man."
Ekphrasis: "The Yellow Books," "Three Acrobats."
Forge: "Madeleine," "Ornate Persona," "Eartheshine."
Medusa's Kitchen: "Balanchine's Woman," "Nature Morte."
North Dakota Review: "Lady and the Unicorn."
Projector Magazine: "Carnival in Rio," "Nijinsky's Afternoon
    of a Faun."
Raven's Tale: "Wild Doll."
Tule Review: "Blue Circus."
Eskimo Pie: "Siddhartha."

Special thanks to William O'Daly, "Poetry in Translation"
class, U. C. Davis, Kazim Ali, Community of Writer's at Squaw
Valley, and Josh McKinney who advised on early versions of
some poems. Special appreciation to Jane Blue, editor of *Tule
Review,* for publishing my first poem, "Blue Circus," 2001.

For my mother, Alice Moon
who gave me my first diary,
and for sewing my first ballet costume by hand.

For my father, Robert Stevens
who gave me my first journal
and my first typewriter, an Underwood Portable.

Things are seldom what they seem.
Skim milk masquerades as cream.

W. S. Gilbert, *H. M. S. Pinafore*

Carnival in Rio

From the film, "Black Orpheus," 1959

Dressed in white cotton,
sweet as blue starch,
she steps from the trolley—
Eurydice in new sandals.

Orfeu's guitar pulls out a bossa nova,
old samba rhythms, feet
thrumming, trying to remember
the location of viper holes.

Revelers burst from ancient frescos.
Jazz hipsters gyrate, ribs
        squeeze and stretch
                like concertinas.

Day collapses—
shops close early.
The man in black, a bone
for a face, skulks in alleyways;
hungry hounds drool and snap.

Eurydice flees to the station,
where snakes strike,
        live cables sting,
and hoist her to heavenly rafters.

After the cruel sunrise,
The Bureau of Missing Persons
gives Orfeu permission
to place her song
among morning's red stars.

Nijinsky's Afternoon of a Faun

Photo Montage
Silent Film Archives, Circa 1915
"Classic Arts Showcase."

1. Costume

Admire my Egyptian eyes, lacquered hair
swirled in place, body taped
like a character doll to reduce curves.
Was it a dream feathering down my neck
or just thoughts, leaf points growing
from the green felt skullcap?

You only see my left side: plum velvet
shoulders, brown grosgrain ribbons
stream warmer than earth,
cover an aquamarine body,
more fish than faun,
shimmering specter, sorcerer,
          harlequin.

2. Choreography

Palms turn up like Krishna's,
cupped hands wait to hold soft love.
See my Valentino grin, broad, luscious,
certain to draw attention?
Small hooves suspend,
barely touch
future projections caught in bas-relief.

I move horizontally, an efficient machine.
Maybe you think me
a pull toy on wheels,
or small kiddy-car locked in track.
Editing resembles a 5-horse powered motor,
limbs well oiled. Lubricant moistens
skin, sweat marks delicate fabric.

Scratching dust,
I look for rubies, dislodge

small stones, release musk,
arch, gyrate,
caress the earthen floor—
not an extreme male legato, just a heart
grinding its way back to dreaming.

3. Nymphs

Forest hues move in panels,
a pull-through diorama: lime green at dawn,
purple as Damson's at midday.

Yesterday, nymphs did not
notice me. Now,
they assume gauzy shapes,
curtains like webbed cauls
divide the hours.

I cannot find one raven curl,
or a single supple pomegranate.
Was that blanched laughter, dry cackle?
Someone mocking? Or my willow flute
grown dry as rustling oat grass?

I grow tired, can no longer feel applause,
or curtsy to receive rosy crowns.

Does anyone remember my profile, spliced,
sealed in still frames? Has anyone heard
my floorboards leaping, releasing iron studded nails?

It's just me—Vaslav

the cloistered somnambulate, withered
limbs, my grand jeté rising
in small alcoves
through two world wars!

Balanchine's Woman

*In my other life, I might be a person
instead of an animal.*
Tanny

      Kicked out of ballet class, she wanted
the hot house of life.

Born angular, a sense of movement, not afraid to use space—
      all space.

In the "Afternoon of a Faun,"
Balanchine could not take his eyes away.
 He loved
  the taste of her
   the sweat of her
     the dance of her
and asked, "Why can't women be faun
to allure, seduce, enchant?"

Too impatient to stand with other dancers
for polio immunizations,
Tanny spent years in Copenhagen's iron lung.
Calm, stay calm. "Did I just touch
        St. Peter's cape?"
Think of the night with small pink clouds.

Years later, somewhat healed, she wondered
     Why is it in art, once you have arrived
     you start to diminish—
then practiced acceptance, forgiveness.

Some asked, "Why Balanchine, why him?"
    "Maybe he just got there first!"

In life, the *Pas de deux* takes many forms.

Lady and the Unicorn

Tapestry, Circa 1600
Musée de Cluny, Paris

Walls run red, the rusty fragrance of first blood.
In deeply woven fabric
she tries to squelch the flow.
No wound, just tart pomegranates
dripping crimson.
Ivory hares and wild raspberries dot a *millefleurs* ground.
Maiden cheeks reflect his milk-white horn.

The guidebook says, "Unicorns are domesticated."
And truthfully, his head rests
in a cushioned lap.
I wonder, who is the seducer,
the most eager to be captured?

A visitor weeps.
Is it the timeless stitching,
craftsmanship, unshod hooves,
or because he is more goat than faun?
Overcome, she wanders
to the gift shop, buys placemats,
25 Euros, a bargain
to hold him under her dinner plate.

A Haibun

*Prince Humay Wounds Princess Humayun in Combat,
the Lovers not Recognizing Each Other.
A Painting, Bihzad c. 1396, Body Colors on Paper*

Her horse paws the ground, knows somethings amiss.
The princess holds hands to the red gash, tiny face
open to a darkened day. Bows lie strewn on the forest floor.
The prince bends down, empty quiver against his thigh.
Her skin: a flesh wound, one drop of blood ?
Yet even the smallest paper-cut stings.

Only last evening, so full of lovemaking, new moon
on her shoulder, scent of sultry lotus. How beautiful the pearl
clasping her scant robe. "Were the flowers too pungent, the ginger
too fresh, too pink, too wet?" At parting, a green creeper grasped
the thin olive, disturbed Humay's mood—harsh words acidic
as tarnished coins. Is *armor* that far from *amour*:
a careless thought, a caress turned rough?

>Above the pine forest
>bright summer evening
>one Dragon weeping

Scarlet flush of circling birds like glassine tears of falling stars

>Phoenix in flight—
>a small garden
>the aging priestess listens

Madeleine

Calligramme, Guillaume Apollinaire

From the small Arabian town
I took a keepsake,
              the memory
of a star pulsating with new fire
engorged on desert heat.

Above clove-scented rooftops,
five points gleamed overlarge
in an azure sky.

              I wanted to fill
my heart with music but
the tender muscle laid open
its boundary for another song.

              Dear Madeleine,
I remember your voice in my ear
like a sprite abuzz
with too many words.

              I apologize
for crossing you out.

The studio portrait I've expected
for so long...arrived today!
On the back: a burnt rose,
twin cannons aflame.

Wild Doll

Joseph Cornell's Bébé Marie

Easy to see she was well fed.
I want to reach in and touch her full cheeks.
Probably a tomboy with those cut bangs
and raised eyebrows.
Easy to see from the expensive dress,
she was found in an estate sale,
a collectible perhaps. Surprising—
as he liked to go cheap: five and dime stores,
thrift shops, items in refuse cans.

Not your ordinary Tiny Tears
or perky Chatty Cathy,
more French porcelain and bisque,
more toddler than baby.
Not cuddled, not coddled.
Not tossed by mice and wind
to suffer dismemberment,
plaid taffeta still bright.

These legs seem right for running,
a brief escape through summer fields.
From the road she sees him,
the quiet, outdoor type.

Playmate come out and play with me.

But all he does is fend off crows,
stand silent on his stick.
In the scent of molding hay, she reverses
steps, still close enough
to grab the trellis to her room.

See her enshrined behind glass,
hiding behind a wicker fence,
field flowers in her hair?

Ornate Persona

Is face the body's icon,
fleshy blue, red, black,
eyes swimming in gold flecks?

Bow lips burnished bronze,
lids violet or sable.
On stalwart stems, face of the rose rests
her head above threadlike roots,
black tangles resemble witches' hair.

The real body—turbulent, defiant heart.
Feelers find their way to epidermis
in grief—wince, sunken eye, pursed lips,
deep crevice, universal grimace,
            universal *prosopon.*

We learn early not to trust masks,
dazzling gems and emerald feathers.
Remember peek-a-boo;
between slit fingers we snuck
a glimpse, a glance?

A mystic once said, "Wear a mask too long—
            find you have no face."

Nature Morte

Sweating pear, wormy cabbage,
      limp rabbit, moldy bread

crystal carafe, leather glove, or peach nude
who will outlive the smaller creatures.

How odd the still life,
everything immobile. Predictable:
                        a permanence

as long as the shriveled petal holds, tuft of fur remains,
fish eye clear and not milky.

Once living: perfumed Bosque, posing hare on the downs,
trout on the Klamath knowing just where to spawn.

We cut up nature to reassemble traces
      of scant memories,

our paint brush creeping black dots of animal spore
into the scenario,

                    kaleidoscope of fin, claw,
stem, root-end dissolved to blue glass and yellow stone.

Is it our nature to rearrange clutter
like the industrious bower bird—
juxtapose contradicting images,
      reorder the universe?

Alabaster woman on a pedestal
bananas bunched and overripe at her feet

nubby oranges, the clumsy rat's
bent nails
caught in a lace shawl.

16

Blue Circus

Marc Chagall

No elephants, bears, or big cats
frame this foreign entertainment,
just a green horse more like a mule,
an emerald chicken beating a drum,
and a sickly blue fish, perhaps a gar.

High above, the lady swings her escape.
Ruby red costume with black jeweled hearts
on ankles and knees. Hair heavy,
topsy-turvy, stage make-up chalky
and bright in primary colors
complete her existence.

Sadly, she belongs here.
Her visions in flight are her life.
They only hold a faded bouquet, more like
cotton wads than flowers,
and a new moon, one eye hanging
on a hook next to a sun
halfway through an eclipse.

A brief glimpse in the cracked canvas
narrowly illuminates places
unknown to her. She began
too young, this vocation,

too late to train
for something else.

Her teeth are missing—
no one will notice.

The Yellow Books

Vincent van Gogh

An empty room, no one here to explain the rich
Arabic print blinds pulled down for the evening.

Yet somewhere light enters. Indented pattern on linen
surges with energy as if made with a curry comb or toy plow.

Stacks of books with crimson bindings gleam as if lit
by ten chandeliers. Tops shimmer with dustings,
wheat light and buttery bee pollen brought in on his coattails.

It is said color effects were mixed by neurological aberrations,
seduced by palettes of Holland's summery landscapes.

Perhaps he drank from the paint-laden water jug instead
of his small flask, the solvent soaking into cracked fingers.
He did not like to wash up for supper.

All volumes remain closed, except for one: a small grey ledger,
a list of years. I think he saved the rest to read when his art
was done, mind at rest, Emeritus.

Six Paintings by Miss X

Commentary
A sequence of poems written in response to paintings by a patient of Carl Jung. It was his contention that healing could take place through artistic expression. After completing the poems, I read Dr. Jung's analysis and selected brief quotes (the epigraphs) I considered expressive of her artwork and my own interpretations.

In the 1920's, an American woman, a psychology major, went to Zurich to continue studies and engage in therapy with Dr. Jung over a ten year period. He called her Miss X. She previously took art classes in Denmark and Dr. Jung suggested she paint her impressions along with their discussions of her dreams.

Of the twenty four numbered paintings, six were selected for this sequence. To me, these represent significant markers in her "liberation," the breaking of "psychological barriers." The titles of the poems are my own. Except for the first two paintings which exhibit rough ovals, all the other twenty two contain versions of the mandala.

Mandala, a Sanskrit word meaning circle, figures in many religious practices as well as dance and prehistoric earthworks. It is considered a symbol for healing, protection and completion: cyclic time, cosmos, even eternity. The design is also evident in dreams and altered states.

My first introduction to the mandala was through meditation where the design may be used to focus attention, where scattered thoughts are brought back to a central point.
I'm also interested in writing from art pieces so naturally was drawn to the paintings.

Six Paintings by Miss X

1. After Midnight

In her imprisoned state, attached to earth.
I advised her not to be afraid of colors.

Overlarge as raptor eggs, boulders pile up
like abandoned children tumbled
from a giant nest.
Captured in gray-brown wash,
they seethe at the core,
a kernel of pale curd.
The central point, a jumble of dark shale,
skirt snagged in brackish water.
She hugs the sharpest
to her chest as if to impale.
A gaunt form, face in darkness,
the only highlight, her blunt-cut hair.
One would think the sea
could lift, hold life, give hope,
but the dull expanse appears firm,
glutinous. Does the sky
hold beauty, a migrating finch
or splash of yellow? If only
she could find a sea star.
Pigment hastily mixed beckons
sandpaper clouds full of grit,
scent of old kelp, soul devoid of spirit.
Her brush wipes out the feeble sun.
Colors seem all of one dun hue
except the trench
wiggling to the horizon,
serpentine, clean, aquamarine.

2. Sphere Abstract

Lightning signifies a sudden, unexpected and
overpowering change of psychic condition.
The patient is replaced by a sphere.

Sun greets trench
sculpts charged bolts
to Z shapes
fractures rock, softens boulders to curvature
like the windshield
of an open-topped convertible seeking directions.

Energy plucks the eye
from a leviathan, the salt-hide
enveloped in such grayness.
Archaic tablet? Blueprint for architecture?

Overlarge and beached,
that eye splits loose, cornea
a red Chinese poppy
last bit of molten magma.

Sharp shoulders sink to granite, take
flange shapes to hold,

guide foundations,
courthouse or temple,
                    warm blood harnessed to earth.

Smooth sea wall rises, early tide
strokes the ragged coastline.

Dandelion dust obliterates grit, the scent
of struck flint, and a softer sulfur
                    from recently lit candles.

3. Hologram

The increase of light indicates conscious realization:
liberation. The sphere... kept afloat by square and
opposite forces...the serpent...
some distance away is aiming down as if to strike.

Sphere blasts to ovum—
   carnelian ripe.

Iron buckle grips girdle,
   like a nipped equator;

inked waves
   divide salt and sky.

Young triangular head
   swathed in gold, shimmers
like a hologram
   unable

to penetrate the smear
   of pink aether.

4. Gorge

Underneath the flower, a small violet...inside
the ovary, indicated by its color, spirit and body.
(Blue+Red). We add to ourselves a bright
and a dark and more night means more light.

Brush mixes neap-tide and celadon foam.
New sea water incubates the quick
leap to throat.
In a tunnel thrashing indigo,
waves suck her skyward.

Seven planets separate in a blue drift,
multiply like the Pleiades
dropping dew on boughs of camphor trees.
Solar rosettes saturate color.
Black diamond divides flaming corona.

Perturbed, the fiery head plunges
barley seeds into a ring;
orange flames split male and female.

She thinks, "Goodbye androgene,
Doric columns, bull-kings and sirens."

Uterine ocean suspends two moons
in a thick crimson wall. She follows
the iron scent of ether's rubber mask.

Last stroke, a golden disc records
her cosmos, a turntable waits for new songs
to be etched. She leaves chaos behind
the blood-brain barrier—and breaks her own.

5. Earthshine

The mandala is suspended over the lit-up ravine
of Fifth Avenue, New York. The blue flower
is the royal pair, King and Queen attended
by an ordinary man and woman.

Clocks read 11:10 P.M. Traffic fills streets:
sedans and delivery trucks travel both directions.

Built of blocks from an old quarry, the city
glistens black with all-night commuters and exhaust.

A waitress on the late shift watches from a window,
a doorman in topcoat guards the entrance.

Cathedral doors are locked, yet lights in the stained
rose window illuminate slender petals of glass flowers.

The new moon, a lily white arc, enfolds Miss X
as she drives the open-topped coupe. Yellow stars

hover over a salt-fragrant bay, the brightest sketching
last night's dream: neon palm, Arabian horse,

oak pulpit, and two green snakes tangled in love.
On fringes, translucent dew resembles children.

Her table is set with dinner plates, a Greek-key
design. The conveniences of long housekeeping?

6. Conch

The mandala floats between Manhattan and the sea…
penetrated by blue snakes into red flesh. The blue
color indicates they have acquired a pneumatic nature.

Out her window, towers
gleam alabaster, yet cathedral doors
open to darkness.

Brilliant carmine spills on Bachelard's words:

"Skyscrapers have no cellars,
    unthinkable for a dreamer of houses."

A Chagall poster inspires.
She adds a small island, abandoned

shack, blue fish, and day star
swaying on a hooked sun.

Sounds of a mermaid's conch,
hair grows long
bright with henna.

Sting of coral on her calf—
she enjoys the wound.

Songs of extinct shore sparrows
fill the horizon.

Clutching velvet bouquets, she considers
the itch, newly formed scales under her thighs.

Why Dancers Wear White
And Some Wear Red

       Because the first flower was white.
Because they are ancient birds. Because
their arms pull comets from the sky.
Because dancing is celestial business.

Because they soar Mesozoic
above the black lake,
trust the buoyancy of air,
the obscure *pirouette,* and
tail feathers shouting the *grand jeté.*

Because they are uncertain if shoulders
will hold in unexpected mist.
They dance to Tchaikovsky
singing like swans toward the sky.

And some wear red, dance
the Merengue, releasing all rhythm,
bony parts jutting free
from delicate clavicles.
The mystery of her body's unknown
strength continues to excite.

Ignore the skilled: the skater
who performs a quad,
the artist who insists on widest borders
for their sketch! She can shout
like the audience, hold molten galaxies

between her limbs, then suddenly appear
at the Moulin Rouge, dance the Can-Can
perform a *ronde jamb!* See patrons
all looking like Toulouse-Lautrec
clapping, stomping on tabletops?

Three Acrobats

Marc Chagall

Curls tight as grommets
she pulls one leg
aloft, reveals four
perfect raspberry breasts,
and round bottom cozy
in fishnet and black sequins.

He ogles her red rhinestones,
in wonderlust holds his privates,
afraid his mascara
and orange pomade will run.
Normally pale from inside work, he feels
a russet vein searing
his neck, a burn the artist captures.

The neutral partner wears gold lamé,
goat head mask and cloven shoes,
arranges locks around horns woven
with white feverfew
smelling of new hay. He hopes his tattoos:
chokecherry clusters, cotton candy stars
            will be noticed.

Thrusting a balsam nosegay
between the others,
he tries to ice them down.
The crowd points
to his polished horns.
He wishes he had chosen a disguise
less obvious, less catchy,
remained an outsider.

The Blueberry Man

This drama borne on jittery air,
like a jack-in-the-pulpit exploding

in early spring. Abrupt retreat,
fleshy stalk shriveled by summer.

You ask what passage will I choose
insist on wearing the gaudy

wig dripping with grapes
and blue-black figs. I'm not fooled

not confused! I see you try
to hide beyond the distant quay.

And yes, perhaps each minute holds
an enchantment. But, this too, can vanish

in just another peeled mango.
I believe in singing and dancing, but

will stay with the calm, apple-cheeked lover
happy at home tending his own orchard.

Siddhartha

Sunday reading, the poet begins:
hydrangeas, sugar water, bugs that transform
to rosary beads; we breathe her rhythm.

After intermission: refreshments.
The person next to me doesn't know the procedure,
slowly chomps cashews,
brazils, keeping time with each meter.

I remember the J Street Theater, long line, "Siddhartha,"
the movie, others comment:
"Saw it in New York, Chicago,
  what a treat, what a trip!"
We bypass popcorn for herbal tea, sink into seats,
the mood set for cypress groves,
lotus flowers, poetry, kisses and song.

  We are India,
arms glowing, cardamom jewels, saffron mums
framed in red paisley, limbs in slow motion.
Mortar and pestle gently grind out
the scent of nutmeg. Moist lips brush brown breasts,
    lovers ascend the tree of desire
        the most erotic scene,
the person behind nervously cracking Jordan Almonds.

The magic gone, Siddhartha quickly
    dissolves
        into a bamboo wood.

I shuffle my poems for open mike,
Are we a feeding species, grazing, nibbling
        air and words together?

Nora has baked Emily D's Party Cake: thick, dark,
spongy, brown sugar, citron, brandy and cloves.

        Siddhartha has a second piece.

NOTES

"Balanchine's Woman." A Found poem, PBS 6/22/14
    Note: Her parents named her Tanaquil,
    after an Etruscan Queen who lived by omens.

"Ornate Persona."
"The face is the icon of creation," John O'Donohue,
Anam Cara: A Book of Celtic Wisdom.
Harper Collins, 1997.

"Six Paintings by Miss X."
Poems in this sequence were inspired by paintings
in *Mandala Symbolism,* C. G. Jung, translated by R.F.C. Hull,
Bollingen Series, Princeton University Press, 1973.

1. "After Midnight," Painting #1
2. "Sphere Abstract," Painting #2
3. "Hologram," Painting #3
4. "Gorge," Painting # 4
5. "Earthshine," Painting #14
    Quote: "The conveniences of long housekeeping,"
    R.W. Emerson, *Emerson on Man and God,* Peter Pauper
    Press, New York, 1961.
6. "Conch," Painting #15
    Quote: *The Poetics of Space,* Gaston Bachelard, translated
    by Maria Jolas, Beacon Press, Boston, 1994.

"The Blueberry Man." A Translitic: "Clair De Lune," Paul Verlaine.

"Why Dancers Wear White," after "Why Performers Wear Black,"
    Desire Lines, Lola Haskins, 2004

Jeanine Stevens is the author of *Limberlost* and *Inheritor* (Future Cycle Press). Her first poetry collection, *Sailing on Milkweed,* was published by Cherry Grove Collections. She is winner of the MacGuffin Poet Hunt, The Stockton Arts Commission Award, The Ekphrasis Prize, and WOMR Cape Cod Community Radio National Poetry Award. *Brief Immensity,* won the Finishing Line Press Open Chapbook Award. Her most recent chapbook, *Gertrude Sitting: Portraits of Women,* won The Heartland Review 2020 Chapbook Award. She participated in Literary Lectures sponsored by Poets and Writers. Work has appeared in *North Dakota Review, Evansville Review, The Kerf, Stoneboat, Rosebud,* and *Chiron Review.* Jeanine studied poetry at U.C. Davis, earned her M.A. at CSU Sacramento, and has a doctorate in Education. She is also a collage artist and has exhibited her work in various art galleries. Jeanine is Professor Emerita at American River College. Raised in Indiana, she now divides her time between Sacramento and Lake Tahoe.

www.ingramcontent.com/pod-product-compliance
Lightning Source LLC
Chambersburg PA
CBHW070957120626
46546CB00004B/1662